The Two Octaves Book
for Viola

Scales

Arpeggios

Broken Thirds

by Cassia Harvey

CHP339

www.charveypublications.com

The Two Octaves Book for Viola
C Major Scale

Cassia Harvey

Broken Thirds in C Major

C Minor Scale

Major/Minor Arpeggios in C

G Major Scale

Broken Thirds in G Major

G Minor Scale

Major/Minor Arpeggios in G

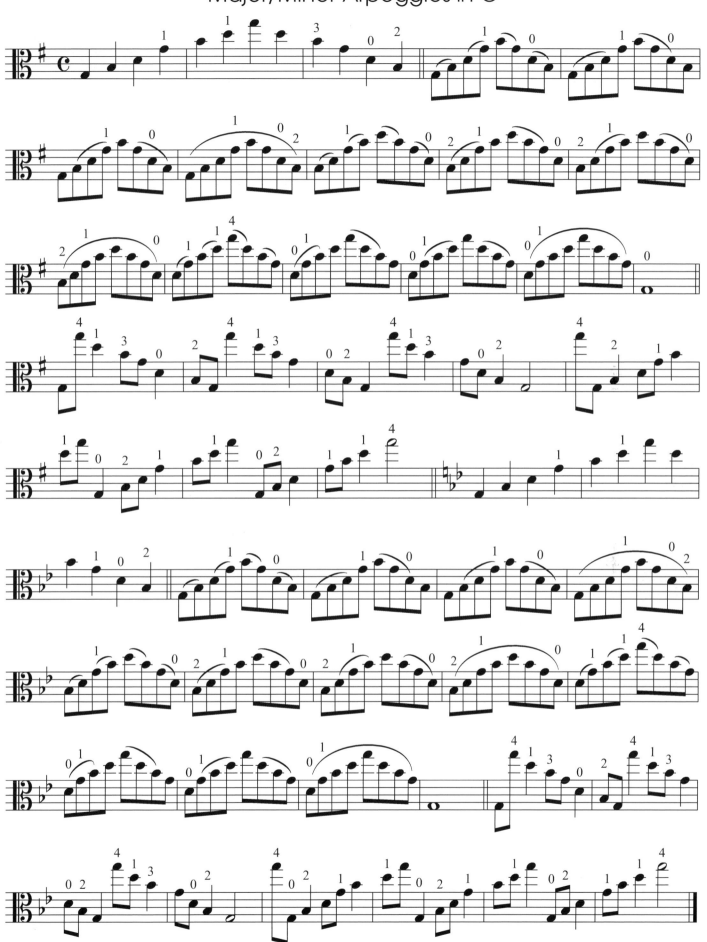

F Major Scale

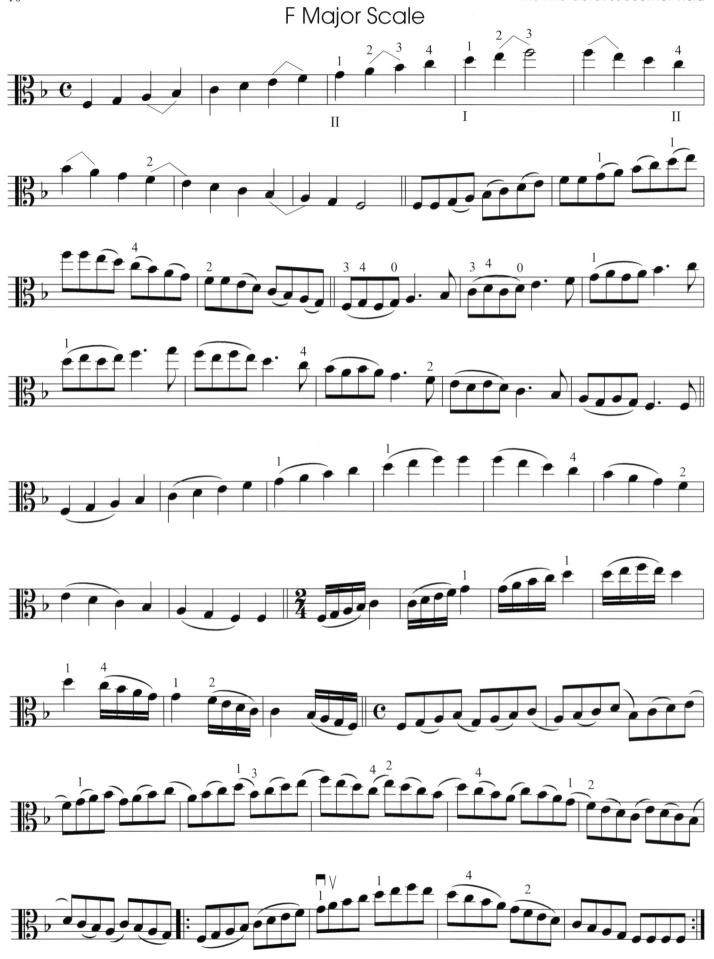

Broken Thirds in F Major

F Minor Scale

Major/Minor Arpeggios in F

D Major Scale

Broken Thirds in D Major

D Minor Scale

Major/Minor Arpeggios in D

B♭ Major Scale

Broken Thirds in B♭ Major

B♭ Minor Scale

Major/Minor Arpeggios in B♭

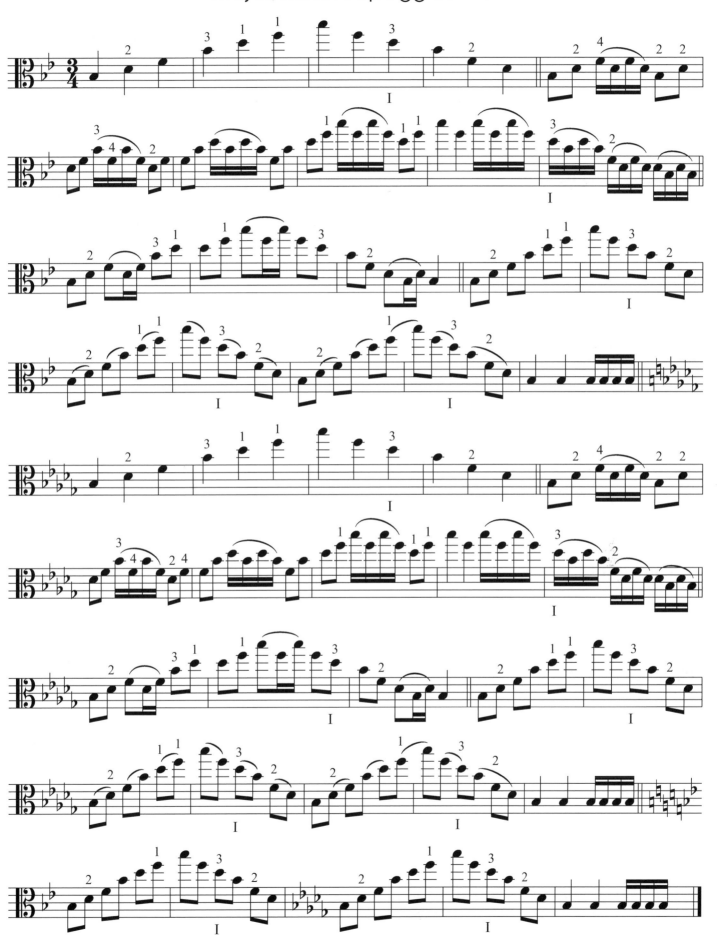

A Major Scale

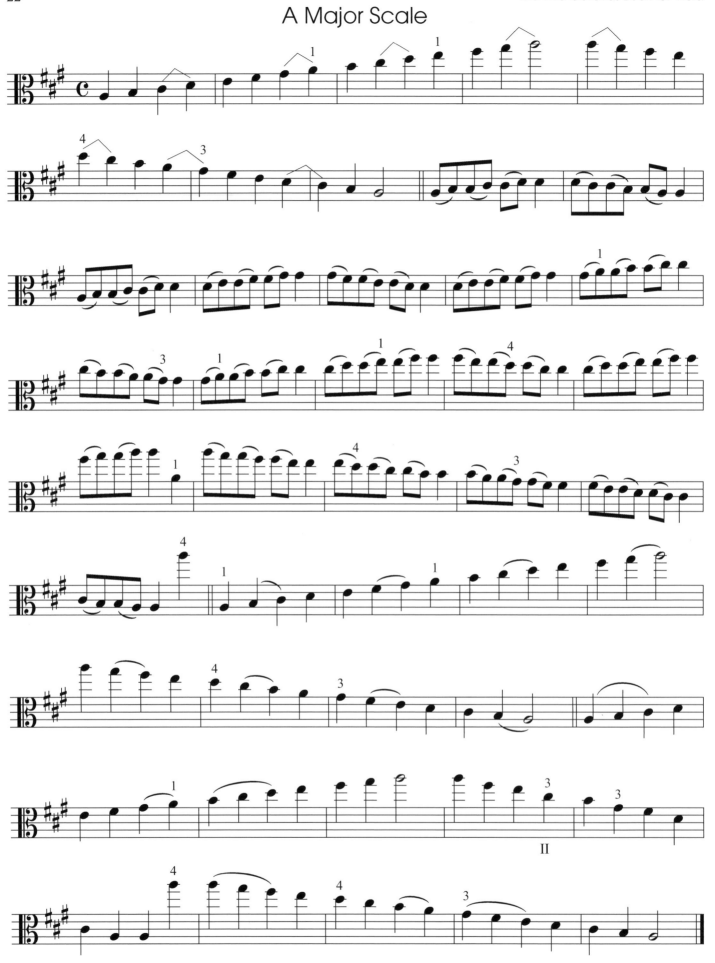

Broken Thirds in A Major

A Minor Scale

Major/Minor Arpeggios in A

E♭ Major Scale

Broken Thirds in E♭ Major

E♭ Minor Scale

Major/Minor Arpeggios in E♭

E Major Scale

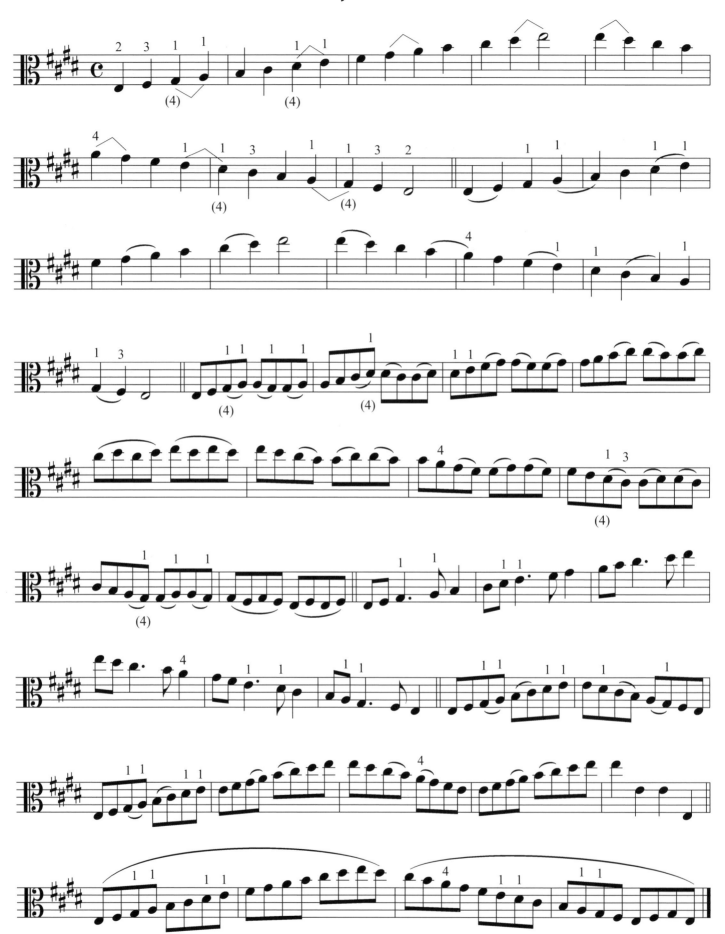

Broken Thirds in E Major

E Minor Scale

Major/Minor Arpeggios in E

A♭ Major Scale

Broken Thirds in A♭ Major

G♯ Minor Scale

Major/Minor Arpeggios in A♭ and G♯

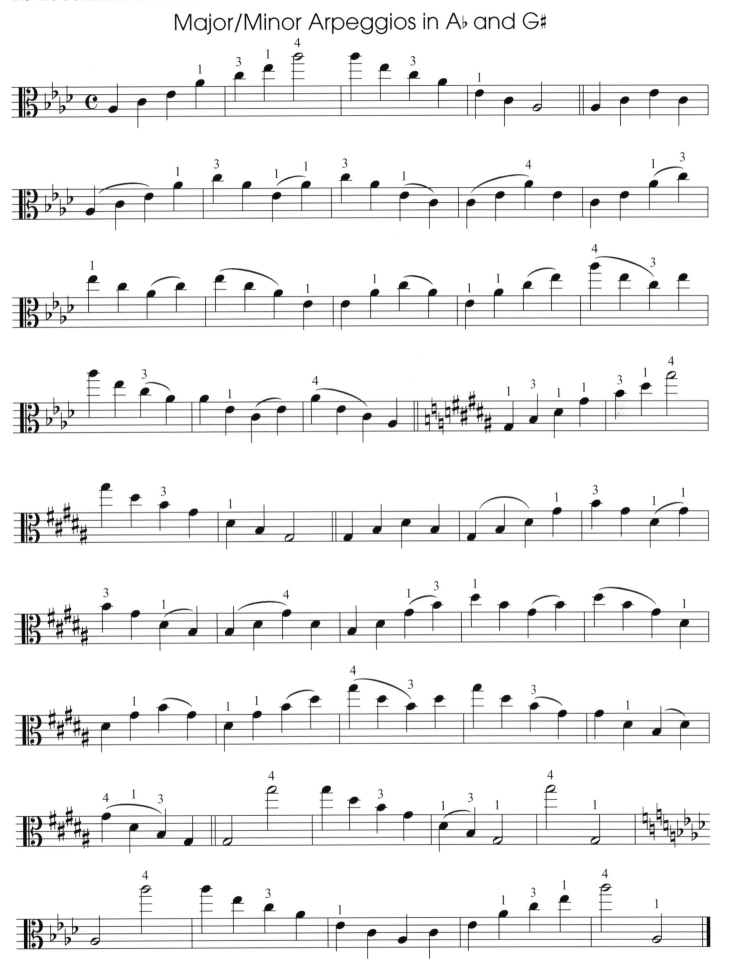

B Major Scale

Broken Thirds in B Major

B Minor Scale

Major/Minor Arpeggios in B

D♭ Major Scale

Broken Thirds in D♭ Major

C# Minor Scale

Major/Minor Arpeggios in D♭ and C♯

G♭ Major Scale

Broken Thirds in G♭ Major

F# Minor Scale

Major/Minor Arpeggios in G♭ and F♯

Chromatic Scales

C chromatic

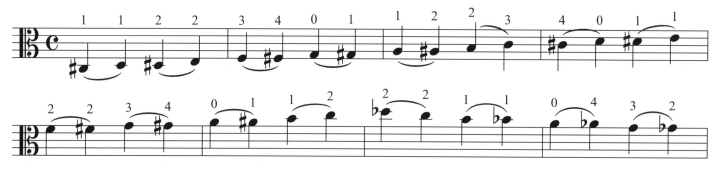

C#/Db chromatic

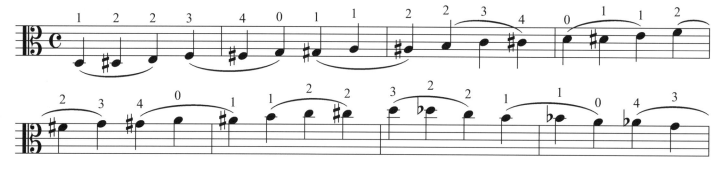

D chromatic

D♯/E♭ chromatic

E chromatic

F chromatic

F♯/G♭ chromatic

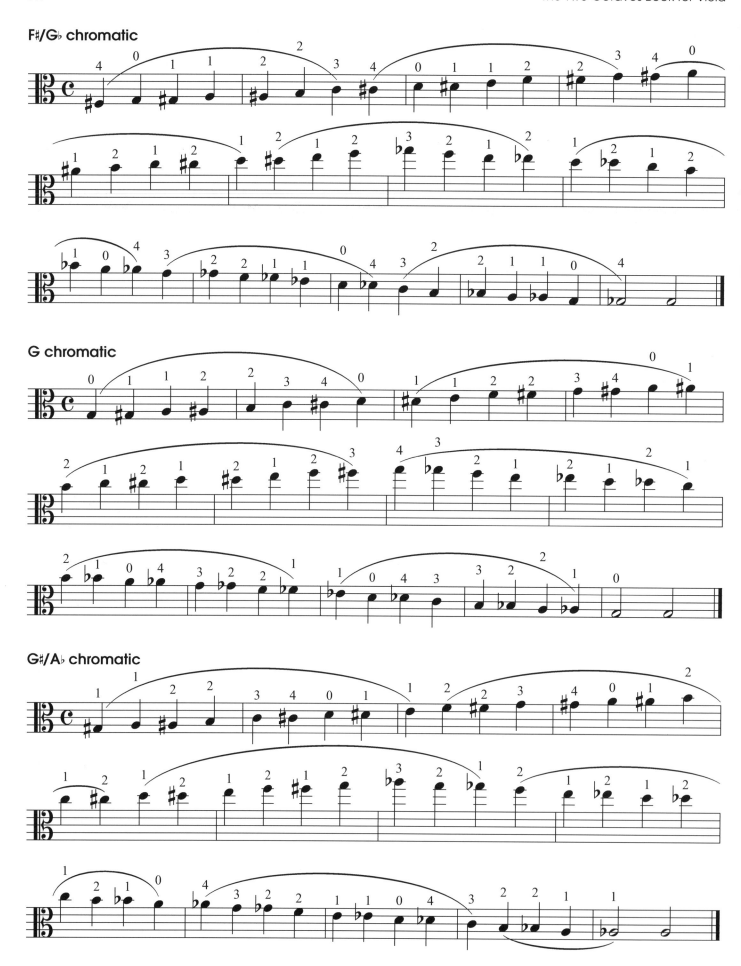

G chromatic

G♯/A♭ chromatic

A chromatic

A#/B♭ chromatic

B chromatic

High C Chromatic

Chromatic Exercise

Harmonic Minor Scales

A minor

E minor

B minor

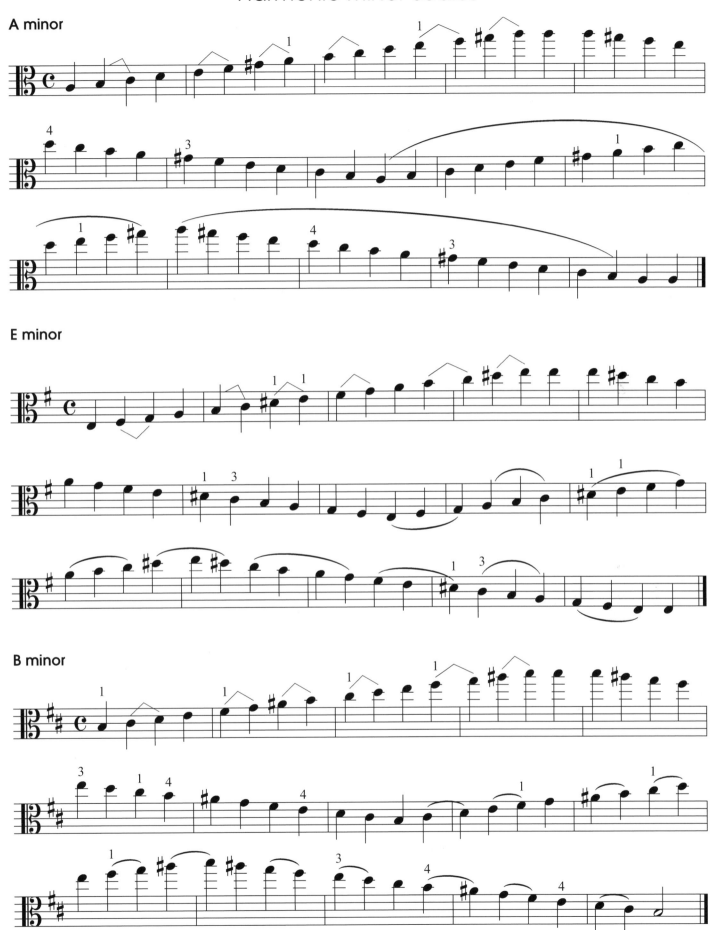

F♯ minor

C♯ minor

G♯ minor

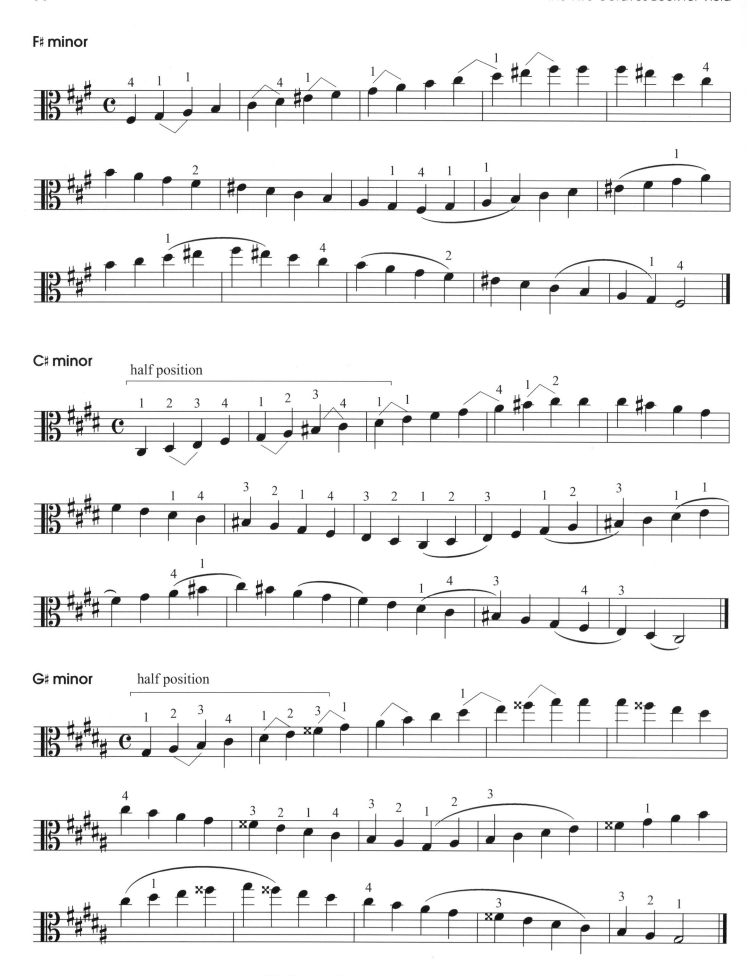

E♭ minor

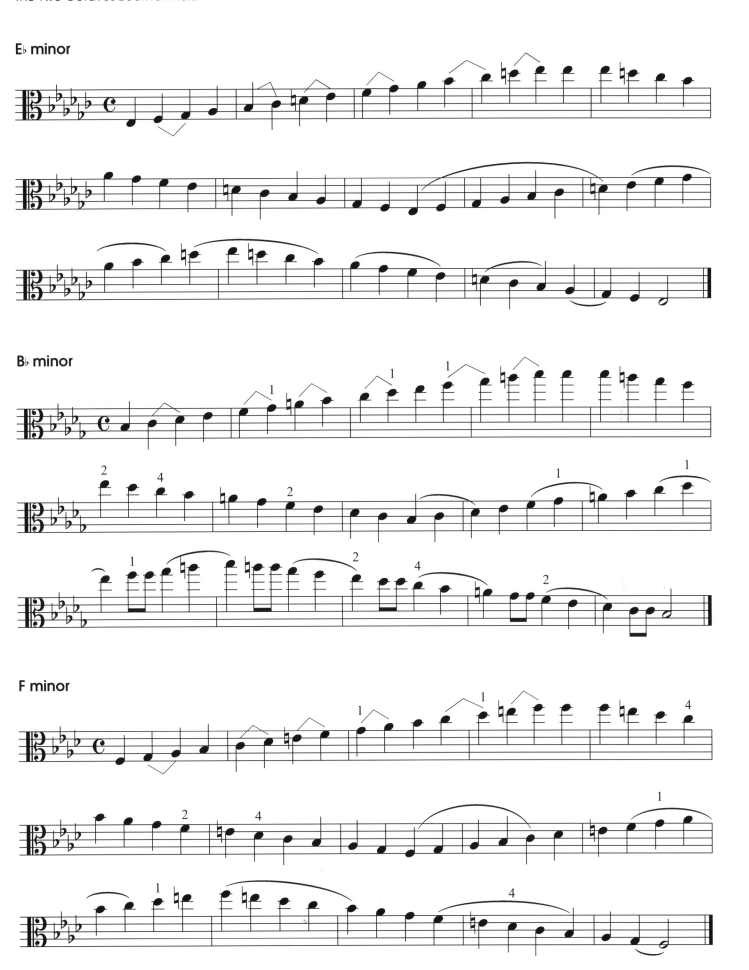

B♭ minor

F minor

C minor

G minor

D minor

Serial Shifting for the Viola

Cassia Harvey

Made in United States
Orlando, FL
05 August 2022